What People Are Saying
by Hank anc

MW00635210

MARKETING FOR PEOPLE WHO THINK THEY DON'T DO MARKETING—If you want a road map to creating a simple but effective marketing plan for your business, this is it. Written in a simple, familiar, breezy, and funny style, this book demystifies the process of establishing, selling, and maintaining your brand and is stuffed full of excellent advice. The highest recommendation I can give is this: I'm an artist. I hate sales and I hate marketing, but this book made me go, "Oh. That's what it is. That's how it works. I guess marketers really aren't evil after all and it's not as hard as I thought it would be." If you're selling something, this book will teach you how to get people to buy it. *–Jon Bastian*

LEARN TO GO FROM CHAOS TO ORDER—If you want to learn anything in this field, Hank is your teacher. *–Mel Powell*

SIMPLY PRACTICAL—This is an excellent book, full of useful tips and insights about marketing. If you own your own business, you'll find many useful examples and ideas to take your business to the next level. Best yet: there's no marketese speak here. The ideas are easy to understand and easy to implement. *—Dan Janal*

As executive director of a non-profit foundation, marketing and fundraising is always a unique challenge. I attended one of Yuloff's marketing seminars and quickly learned how much I needed to learn. So, I anxiously awaited the release of this book. I now have my Marketing Bible. Great ideas, great suggestions! *—Kathleen Hale*

A MUST-READ MARKETING BOOK! Yet another fabulous marketing book from Hank & Sharyn Yuloff! Their tips & ideas on effective social media marketing are excellent. So glad I bought this book! *—Cynthia Lay*

GREAT MARKETING TIPS—There's always room for improvement on marketing your message as a business owner. Hank and Sharyn Yuloff make it fun and easy to up your game and focus on what works. —*Wil Bowers*

ANSWERS ALL YOUR QUESTIONS! Excellent! Clear! Pertinent! Helpful! And, entertaining! If you are floundering and want a way to tackle social media, THIS IS YOUR BOOK! —*Joia Jitahidi*

Great Book! I have been in the marketing field so some of this stuff I already knew, but even with my experience I picked up quite a few nuggets that I've already implemented into my business. —*Jack Stone*

This is a smart book for anyone looking for a working proven system for success. —*Craig A. Valine*

I was absolutely thrilled when I learned Hank Yuloff had penned this book. He did a brain dump of his three decades of marketing knowledge. A business owner or independent contractor would be foolish not to have this marketing bible on their desk. Hank has made it easy for you to apply strategies that flat out work. This is a solid HOW TO! Don't pass this one up. You can't afford NOT to own this book. —*Joseph Buzello*

WONDERFUL BOOK WITH COUNTLESS TIPS TO BOOST YOUR BUSINESS—I applied just a couple of tips and I'm receiving more clients. —*Nargas*

SMALL BUSINESS HUMAN RESOURCES SECRETS

The Right Way to Hire, Cultivate and Terminate Employees, All While Improving Your Marketing

HANK AND SHARYN YULOFF

SMALL BUSINESS HUMAN RESOURCE SECRETS

SMALL BUSINESS HUMAN RESOURCE SECRETS

The Right Way to Hire, Cultivate,

and Terminate Employees,

All While Improving Your Marketing

Hank and Sharyn Yuloff

Naked Book Publishing

Any examples, stories, references, or case studies are for illustrative purposes only and should not be interpreted as testimonies and/or examples of what reader and/or consumers can generally expect from the information. No representation in any part of this information materials and/or seminar training are guarantees or promises for actual performance. Any statements, strategies, concepts, techniques, exercises and ideas in the information, materials and/or seminar training offered are simply opinion or experience, and thus should not be misinterpreted as promises, typical results or guarantees (expressed or implied). The author and publisher (Henry "Hank" Yuloff, Sharyn Yuloff, Naked Book Publishing nor any of their representatives) shall in no way, under any circumstances, be held liable to any party (or third party) for any direct, indirect, punitive, special, incidental or other consequential damages arising directly or indirectly from any use of books, materials and/or seminar trainings, which is provided "as is," and without warranties.

PRINTED IN THE UNITED STATES OF AMERICA

This book is dedicated to our parents who always encouraged us to pursue each of our career ambitions and to collaborate whenever possible.

Contents

Special <u>FREE</u> Bonus Gift for <u>YOU!</u>

To help you achieve more success, there are **FREE BONUS RESOURCES** for you at:

YourBonusGift.com

FREE SOCIAL MEDIA CONTENT PLUS
A FREE SOCIAL MEDIA TRAINING DAY VIDEO
which is part of Hank and Sharyn's very successful entrepreneurial marketing program:

The Small Business
MARKETING
PLAN
.COM

The Small Business Marketing Plan is a new type of hybrid do-It-Yourself WITH Coaching program that allows small business owners like you to learn the right way to promote their business and increase sales. It begins with teaching you how to create your ideal target market and then speak to them the right way. **The Social Media Training Day** video is a bonus offered to business owners who invest in their business with the Plan. And now it is being given to YOU.

FREE $1997 VALUE

Get started now at

YourBonusGift.com

xvii

A Message to You!

After spending over fifteen years in human resources in Southern California, I thought Hank was the only one of us who understood marketing. However, after spending a year on disability with a work-related injury and overhearing his conversations with his clients, I realized that our conversations were not so different. In fact, it seems to me that HR in a small business is actually *internal* marketing: I was either marketing the employee to the employer, or the employer to the employee.

The only exception, of course, is when I had to place an ad for a new employee, in which case it truly was external marketing.

I also learned that California is a very employee-friendly state, probably the friendliest state of all. Therefore, if you comply with California employment law, you are probably in compliance in your state. However, I must insist that you check with your local employment law attorney or professional employer organization (PEO) if you are partnered with one.

Hank spent six years as a sales manager for two different organizations. He approaches human resources from the unique point of view of the sales department for a company which must balance what is best for the employee and what is best for the company's sales profitability.

Most of this book is from the point of view of human resources and logically it is me talking to you, but there are places where Hank jumps in— we tag team just as we do in our presentations and consulting.

The recommendations throughout this book should only be used as guidelines. Please only select the portions that apply to your company. Neither the author nor YuloffCreative.com will assume legal liability for the accuracy, completeness, or usefulness of any information provided in whole or in part within this publication.

Sharyn Yuloff, MBA

Preface

"Coaching is unlocking a person's potential to maximize their own performance. It's helping them to learn rather than teaching them."
Tim Gallwey, Sports Methodology Coach

"A coach is someone who tells you what you don't want to hear, who has you see what you don't want to see, so you can be who you always knew you could be."
Tom Landry, NFL Hall of Fame Coach

We are business coaches for highly motivated entrepreneurs just like you. We are Sharyn and Hank Yuloff, partners of Yuloff Creative Marketing Solutions.

For most people, the three hardest areas to control and improve their business are the areas where we focus: your marketing messaging, your sales abilities, and your human resources and relationships. In those areas we work for you, create for you, think for you, and figure it all out for you. We create a custom business coaching package that looks at deeper fundamentals of your business, such as your business model, your operations, your profit margins, and your marketing plan. We also interview, hire, create, and train your team and place you on a more profitable path to success.

On the sales side of every business, it's not always so easy to excel because while you were taught how to *do* what you do, rarely are we taught how to *market* or *sell* what we do.

For that part of your business, we are the bridge between where you are in your business to the vision you have for your life. We take what you have as a vision and develop the plan to get you there. Then, using the right tactics, direct your message to the potential clients of your dreams, and put you on the path to the life you envision.

In this book, as with all our books, we are trying to help you get better at one of the hardest part of your business, human resources. You will get the basics that will make your job easier and for the rest you can come to us at www.FreeHRConsultation.com.

We are here to think for you, work for you, and figure it all out for you.

Chapter 1

Finding Your Team AKA Recruiting

Employees or Candidates: What Are You Really Looking For?
The first advice I share with hiring managers is to look for candidates that have the necessary skills to provide the deliverables that the role requires. Let's define *deliverables* as the total skills needed to perform the job at an above average level. Another way of putting this is that as the owner of the company, an employee is delivering more value by their work, than it costs to pay them. The number that you use to multiply by the cost to pay them is going to be a consideration you take into account with every hiring or firing decision. You want to hire good employees, not good candidates. Many people can interview well yet cannot produce the required deliverables.

We get asked all the time, "What about using interns?"

If you are looking to fill an entry-level role, I strongly encourage you to consider using a college intern who is eager to work in their chosen field for low wages *and* college credit. With rare exception, gone are the days when *intern* means free labor.

Would hiring a consultant be the answer?

If you are looking to fill a role that requires expertise, but does not require full time employment, I often encourage exploring a consultative arrangement. However, since too many employers were seen to be taking advantage of this arrangement, HR laws have become quite strict. The key point in deciding if the arrangement can remain consultative is if the role requires specific employer-mandated procedures or employer-mandated hours. If the role is more project based and can be completed by an individual at their convenience and at their chosen locale, then a consulting arrangement should work. I do strongly advise that you work with your employment law attorney on an as-needed basis to prepare and review all consulting agreements. You can find some guidance through the IRS website, specifically https://

1

www.irs.gov/businesses/small-businesses-self-employed/independent-contractor-self-employed-or-employee and the Department of Labor website: https://www.dol.gov/WHD/regs/compliance/NewBus3.pdf

Where Are the Candidates Hiding?

Gone are the days when employers can put out an ad in their local paper and wait for candidates to line up. That's mostly because newspapers are getting less common. However, the days may also be numbered for the numerous online job boards as well. As of this writing, two of the most effective places to find your ideal employee are LinkedIn and Facebook.

Post Where They Are Looking

As with all social media endeavors, I encourage hiring managers to post their job opportunities wherever their ideal employee is looking. If your ideal employee is more professional than social, LinkedIn may be your best bet. However, if your ideal employee is younger and the role requires more visual stimulation, you may find her on Instagram. Basically, our advice is to not limit yourself to the stereotypical job boards where everyone else is posting, but rather to be seen wherever your ideal employee is lurking.

Network Where Your Ideal Employee Is Meeting

I advise hiring managers to physically go to wherever their ideal employee is networking. For example, if you are looking for a social employee who is committed to community service, I would advise exploring your local chamber of commerce as well as other local non-profit organizations. If you have funds available to relocate your ideal employee, then you may want to travel to their local venues rather than look in yours. It all depends on who and where your ideal employee is as well as your available funds. There are also several websites which offer opportunities for people who enjoy similar things to gather for meetings, for example, MeetUp.com. If there are particular skills that are needed, you may find her there.

Ask Your Friends and Employees

You may want to spread the word through your personal and professional network. Some of our best hires (and honestly, worst, so take care) were the result of referrals.

Sorting
Application Review

It has become common practice to require an application for every employment role, because it provides an easy way for the employer to screen for specific needs (such as language proficiency) and screen out specific issues (such as criminal history). With the use of an employment application, the employer can easily advise candidates of some important requirements such as hours and travel without having to rely on the hiring manager to consistently advise each candidate of these policies. This is also an easy way to obtain the necessary releases for background and reference checks so that a top candidate is not alerted to their position in the sorting process before the employer is truly ready to divulge such information.

Resumé Review

It has become common practice to advise hiring managers to *not* make notes or any stray marks on any resumé as these can be subpoenaed and used against an employer if a candidate suspects discrimination. Some employers utilize a scoresheet which is retained separately from the resumés and discarded once a role is fulfilled. A sample scoresheet can be found in Appendix A of this book.

Hank has used the resumé as a reason to spot trouble prior to the interview process. He was interviewing salespeople for jobs in the advertising world where they would be responsible for creating ads. If a word was misspelled in an ad, it would cost his company money for a reprint. If he saw misspellings in a resumé, that was always an immediate flag that this person would probably not take care in their work for a client, either. In this way, Hank was looking for reasons to *not* go through the interview process with a candidate who could cause the company to have a lower bottom line.

Cover Letter Review

The use of cover letters has become increasingly scarce as more employers switch to digital reviews. The primary exception to this is for roles that require significant written communication. In those instances, cover letters can be a key tool in distinguishing one candidate from another.

Cover letters let us check the writing ability of our prospective employees. The written word will always be an important method of communication, and the cover letter is an important screening process.

It is always fine to ask a candidate why they chose your ad, or what about your company specifically caused them to respond. Figure out what makes them want to speak to you, and you may be able to shorten the interview time. This is one way you can find better candidates instead of someone who is simply hitting a send-resumé button to a thousand companies.

Interviewing
Phone Interviews
I strongly suggest using a phone interview as the first step in narrowing down a hiring manager's selection. This is the time to have a consistent set of questions that is asked of each candidate to avoid the appearance of discrimination. It is also a way to limit unnecessary hours of personal interviews since phone interviews tend to be much quicker. Another reason is because this process can be more easily delegated either to your HR staff or a trusted assistant. A sample phone interview template can be found in Appendix B.

Hank's favorite two questions were, "What do you know about our industry?" and "Why do you want to sell our product?" If he received a "not much" and "well, selling is selling and I can sell anything" answer, he knew that they had not done any research and if they had, they would have realized quickly that "selling is not selling" and his products required a creative skillset.

Personal Interviews
As an HR Manager/Director, I reserve the in-person interviews for the top ten percent of candidates screened during the phone interview process. As the HR delegate, I still preferred to meet with the candidate first, before passing them up to the hiring manager. More than once, a candidate that seemed to be top notch during the phone interview, quickly became disqualified during the first few minutes of an in-person meeting. It is far more cost-effective and efficient to waste the time of your HR personnel or administrator than it is the hiring manager who is often at a much higher pay scale.

This is often the reason the HR delegate has been hired as an HR screener, they get through prospects much faster. They can tell who the prospects are who will market your business as well as doing the job they are hired to perform.

Group Interviews
As much as I dislike being the potential employee in a group interview situation, as the HR representative I advocate for them as much as possible, for some obvious reasons:
- This style is highly uncomfortable for most candidates and thus allows those of the highest caliber to truly shine.
- This style is also highly efficient because multiple members of the

team can meet with the candidate at the same time at the employer's site without the candidates being passed along from one key employee to another.

- This style provides key personnel a chance to see how each candidate will fit in with the team in their regular conference setting.
- If you are attempting to build a corporate culture, you can include people from the department that the candidate will work in, so the current employees can see that their opinions matter and are appreciated.

When Hank was preparing to interview sales people for the first time, he and his assistant advertising manager compiled a list of questions they were going to ask. If one of them was done with that potential employee they would jump further down the list of questions. If the other disagreed, they would jump back up. This was a way they could have a conversation within a conversation. They noticed that after going through this process several times, there was little disagreement because they had set very definite guidelines prior to the interviews about the type of sales professional they wanted on their team and their questions were created to find the people who would fit in the best.

Prioritizing

This is also known as *rating the applicants*. After each candidate has been interviewed, I recommend revisiting the resumé scoresheet as adjustments may need to be made. If this is done after each interview, it becomes much easier to narrow down the candidate options to your top three choices to fill any particular role.

Chapter 2

Inking Your Team

Due Diligence

Background checks: It is still inappropriate for an employer to search through a candidate's social media profile and online presence. However, it is still commonly performed. If a potential candidate puts their social media links on a resumé, then it is an invitation that should not be ignored.

It is, however, highly recommended to outsource a full background check, including online presence, and criminal and financial records. Since these can become quite costly, I do suggest that they only be performed on those candidates you are seriously considering hiring. Additionally, I recommend differing levels of background checks, depending on the needs of each given role. For example, a front desk administrator that does not handle any employer finances may not require a credit report while those that work in finance, accounting and the c-suite most certainly do.

Reference checks: This, too, is a potential sticky situation. Although all smart candidates will only include contact information for those in their circle that they can trust will provide a good reference, it is still wise to call them because you never know. I would hate to be in the position of thinking *if only I had known* when my supervisor asked if I had called the references and I had responded, "Oh, no, those are never worthwhile." My key ninja trick is to look at the candidate's prior employers and see if there is anyone I or the hiring manager know at those companies, even if they are not who the candidate wrote down as the contact person. Here's the issue with reference checks: As our culture becomes more litigious (if that's even still possible), fewer employers are willing to say much more than to confirm a candidate's dates of employment, title, and compensation. But, again, I would hate to be in a position of, "If only I had called and found out that they were lying on their resumé and had never actually worked there."

Making the Offer

Once the hiring manager has decided on their first, and maybe second choice, my standard practice is to provide the hiring manager with a draft offer letter to ensure that both parties are in agreement on what is being offered. Then I advise the hiring manager to call the candidate to extend a verbal offer, using the draft offer letter as their guide. While it is possible for the HR personnel to make this call, the candidate is much more likely to accept the initial offer if it is made by the hiring manager directly because they will feel a more personal connection to their potential supervisor. Once the candidate and hiring manager have agreed on the key points of the offer, the hiring manager should provide those details to human resources to complete the formal offer letter and then give it to the hiring manager, or the appropriate personnel (such as CEO, COO, or President) for signature.

Below are the key components of most standard offer letters, with a formal example in Appendix C.

- Compensation (both the amount and the pay check schedule)
- Possible relocation expenses
- Reporting hours and start date
- Full or part time status
- Dress code
- Benefits (such as health, vacation, education, expense account)
- Introductory period (*not* probation): It is imperative, at least in California at the time of this writing, that the introductory period not be stated as probation. Most employment in this state is *at will*, meaning either party may terminate the arrangement at any time, for any legal reason, and without notice. As such, there is no distinction between the first ninety days and any other period of employment. However, it is also understood that the first few weeks is the time when a new employee is becoming acclimated to their new role and a new corporate culture. As such, a little leniency is expected except for clearly egregious errors. If these few weeks are stated as *probationary*, it becomes far more difficult to uphold the *at-will* status.

Use the following link for more information: https://resources.workable.com/formal-offer-letter-template

Negotiating

Remember the old adage that it is far more expensive to obtain a new customer than it is to keep a current one? The same is true for employees. As such it is imperative that negotiations always occur in good faith, and especially before a formal offer letter is presented.

New Employee's First Day—Orientation

As you recall, part of the offer letter is the agreed upon first day, reporting time, and reporting location. I highly recommend alerting all personnel of a new employee's start date, time, and role so that the new employee gets a warm welcome. This starts with the front desk staff. My standard operating procedure is to have the front desk greet the new employee as if they were welcoming a distant relative (make them feel welcome, and yet at home, not a guest). Have reception escort them to human resources, or have HR greet them at the reception area (this depends upon the layout of your office space and the ability of the front desk administrator to be removed from the post for the welcome). Since there are typically many forms to be completed and discussed, this is the best place for a new employee to start. Once the documentation process is complete, HR can then walk with the new employee to their desk, introducing them to the team as they are each encountered, and providing a tour of the facilities at the same time. Once they arrive at their desk, the new employee can be handed off to the hiring manager for continued role-specific orientation.

We also suggest a quick pop-in during the day by human resources just to make certain things are going smoothly and to remind them that the door is always open for questions.

Chapter 3

Benefits (The Things That Get Them in the Door and Keep Them in the Building)

Below is a list of some of the most common benefits that HR will review with each new employee as part of the orientation conversation. While some are obvious, others seem to warrant more explanation, which I have provided below.

Health Insurance

This has become more complex with the passage and implementation (and the mass changes of the Affordable Care Act—Obamacare), including recent Supreme Court rulings.

When establishing your employee benefit plan consider the following:
- Health insurance
- Vision insurance
- Dental insurance
- Domestic partners/spouses—what is provided for them
- Flexible benefits: This is defined as "A benefit program that offers employees a choice between various benefits including cash, life insurance, health insurance, vacations, retirement plans, and child care. Although a common core of benefits may be required, you can choose how your remaining benefit dollars are to be allocated for each type of benefit from the total amount promised by the employer. Sometimes you can contribute more for additional coverage. Also known as a Cafeteria plan or IRS 125 Plan." These allocated funds are pretax dollars. (*See* https://www.healthcare.gov/glossary/flexible-benefits-plan)
- Wellness and preventative care

Ancillary Coverage

You can sweeten the pot for your employees with additional benefits. The most commonly provided coverages are:

- AFLAC (or policies like it): These insurance policies provide payment to the employee as per the specific coverage, thereby assisting the employee in meeting their financial obligations while being treated, without any cost to the employer. This is a voluntary benefit that the employee can either choose to pay for or not.
- Employee Assistance Program (EAP): This is typically provided as part of the health benefits so that there is no cost to the employer or the employee, and yet is available to the employee for such stressful events as the death of their spouse, a terminal illness diagnosis, helping aging parents, and mental health issues.
- Disability: This benefit is provided by the state and can also be provided as supplementary coverage of a health-care policy, if an employee becomes injured, either on or off the job.
- Long-term care: As we continue to watch our parents age, more of us are considering this supplemental coverage that helps to alleviate some of the financial burden from our estate.
- Tuition assistance: This is particularly helpful for those employees that are interested in pursuing additional education, especially as it relates to their role while employed by you.

Financial Planning Services

This is an area where I advise caution, especially if the employer offers a profit sharing plan or stock options. My specific suggestion is to retain a third-party administrator in order to avoid any semblance of impropriety or bias. Things to consider are:

- 401k: This is the most commonly found benefit offered in the financial services arena, but certainly not the only. It is named for the IRS code that governs these types of accounts. (*See* http://www.irs.gov/Retirement-Plans/401(k)-Plans)
- ERISA (The Employee Retirement Income Security Act of 1974): This is the federal law that governs most employee benefits. (*See* http://www.dol.gov/dol/topic/health-plans/erisa.htm)
- Life insurance: This benefit is typically offered in conjunction with health benefits. It is typically limited and thus may only supplement an employee's existing coverage. (*See* http://www.bizfilings.com/toolkit/

sbg/office-hr/managing-the-workplace/life-insurance-as-an-employ-ee-benefit.aspx)

Paid Time Off

Maintaining accurate records of an employee's time away from the office can be quite cumbersome, especially for the most senior members of a team who are often out of the office on business and do not like to be questioned by human resources as to the nature of their absence. The most common non-work-related absences are for illness (either personal or a loved one) and vacation. Many employers are instituting a paid-time-off policy that does not distinguish as to the nature of the absence, provided it is *not* work related. This eliminates some record-keeping issues as well as the need for an employee to "call in sick" even when they simply have personal matters to attend to for at least part of a work day. Paid time off is usually used for sick time and vacation time. Eligibility for sick time is one hour accrued for every thirty hours worked as of July 1, 2015.

When it comes to benefits, remember that this is one aspect of employment that a candidate will likely share with friends. If you can add fun benefits such as once a year, the team gets together for a picnic in the park and then goes home early, it can help your company stand out as an inviting place to work. We will discuss this in more detail in the next chapter.

Chapter 4

Keeping the Best of Your Team— Employee Retention

Keeping Your Team Engaged

Most employees are the most engaged their first week of employment. Maintaining that level of engagement can be difficult for many employers. As one becomes more accustomed to their role, some employees become disengaged from the larger corporate efforts and narrow their focus to only their role and those with whom they interact most often. There are many ways in which an employer can create an environment that promotes a contented workplace for their employees.

Team Building

In an ideal world, each corporate team would focus at least part of a day each quarter on building the team, however that is defined. For some smaller employers, this may mean a full corporate shut down for at least a few hours, or it may mean only a specific department is inaccessible for a few hours on a rotating basis. For one small employer based in Santa Monica, California, this meant a day at the beach each summer where we played volleyball and enjoyed some personal time with our colleagues away from the office.

Employers with more substantial sales teams may utilize sales contests to motivate sales teams to compete as well as cooperate. For example, one employer created individual, team, and whole business goals based on sales volume that allowed individuals, sales managers, and the entire company to benefit based on differing levels of achievement.

There was a direct mail company that Hank worked for which always tried to make their company-wide sales meetings fun. They would gather for an hour of work, then an activity, then finish the day with awards. One day they rented out a go-cart facility, another time a dramatic home overlooking the ocean (with limo service from each location for the sales leaders).

We also used to run contests for our teams competing against other parts of the country. The winners would get prizes such as electronics or bonuses. Most of our contests revolved around winning prizes. Our favorite was the opportunity to win a cruise for the top ten percent in the sales department, or one hundred percent in sales growth, year over year. The entire company got involved because for each person who won a cruise in the sales department, a home office person would be chosen to go as well. Twenty-five percent of the company ended up being on the ship.

There was another contest where we had the chance to earn a case of steaks for selling a certain amount of one product. The company registered a thirty percent growth in sales of that product, which continued for the next two years.

For our own company, we have begun running a contest for our private coaching clients. We have fifteen to twenty ways they can earn points and the top earner each year wins prizes including a stay in our private suite for Alumni Weekend (a coaching program for all clients, past and present) plus extra private time masterminding with us to build their business.

Conflict Resolution
This is one of the more challenging roles for human resources, though it can be quite rewarding for those that find they have a knack for it. In my experience, most conflicts were between colleagues who somehow felt slighted. However, occasionally the issue was between the manager and the subordinate and was deemed to be part of the termination process.

"People do not quit their jobs, they quit leaders."
Larry Broughton

Retaliation
This can be a difficult issue for some employers who feel the urge to exact revenge for a conflict. However, it is imperative that all employees be provided an arena to raise conflicts and work on their positive resolution without being concerned for their job security.

Attendance
One clue that an employee is becoming disengaged is an increase in tardiness and/or absenteeism. With careful monitoring, HR should be able to alert management to any relevant change in an employee's attendance in an effort to mitigate an unnecessary departure and/or termination.

Complaints

Employee engagement can be hampered by both internal and external complaints. Internal complaints have been discussed above under conflict resolution. However, external complaints, those brought to management's attention by a client or customer, can also be devastating for some employees and create a break in their corporate engagement.

Investigations

One role of a human resources department is to lead investigations of employee misconduct. Since there are some very specific rules about how investigations are to be performed, many employers retain a third-party consultant to perform the investigations, which also provides a semblance of arms' length removal for both the employer and for HR. (*See* http://www.shrm. org/publications/hrmagazine/editorialcontent/2011/0511/pages/0511legal. aspx)

Emergency Planning

This role may fall to the office manager, though typically it is performed in conjunction with HR since employees will need to know where to go and what to do in the event of an emergency. This is a fantastic opportunity for team building. Everyone's input can be solicited. An emergency organizer can be designated to assist the manager in a department.

Emergency Supplies

In my experience, obtaining emergency supplies can be easily delegated to an HR administrator or the office manager. Employee engagement often increases when emergency preparations are taken seriously by the employer because employees note the care and importance that their safety is given.

Telecommuting

Although it is difficult for managers and HR to monitor telecommuting employees, for some employees, engagement does increase because they appear to be trusted. However, for other employees, engagement decreases as they feel less a part of the organization.

Job Descriptions

One of the keys to maintaining employee engagement is accurately matching the job description to the role the employee is performing. While this can be initially done by human resources in conjunction with the hiring manager, monitoring continued accuracy requires employee involvement.

Job Analysis

I typically recommend that a job description analysis be performed at each annual employee review. This provides the employee, their manager, and HR the opportunity to evaluate if the job for which the employee has been retained is actually the job the employee is performing. It is surprising how much a role can morph from the original retention description with the specific skills each individual can bring to a role. Since most of my employment was with small businesses, I often stressed during the recruitment process that the role I may create in a position may be quite different from the role John Doe may create even in the same position. An employee who feels that their growth and input is valuable to their supervisor and their employer is unsurprisingly more engaged than an employee who feels they must stay within the box for which they were initially retained.

Mentoring

Traditional mentoring has some specific guidelines. However, even a casual mentoring relationship can increase employee engagement for both the *mentor* and the *mentee*. A mentorship program can be encouraged at any stage, though it is typically seen at the beginning of employment or anytime an employee may be having difficulties. This encourages retention rather than separation.

Moonlighting

Unsurprisingly, employees that hold another, non-competing job openly, are typically more engaged than those that are required to do so under subterfuge.

Corporate Events

Much like team building activities, corporate events and parties can be a way to increase employee morale because it provides a venue to socialize with colleagues outside of the work environment.

Paying Your Team

It is admittedly difficult to retain your team if you do not provide sufficient and consistent compensation. However, it is important to remember that there are several parts to compensation beyond the hourly wage or weekly salary.

Compensation

Of course, the first piece is indeed the hourly wage or weekly salary that was agreed upon in the original offer letter and subsequently modified as part of any appropriate review process.

Payroll

While the creation and maintenance of an appropriate compensation structure does typically start with HR in conjunction with a senior member of the financial staff, it is not unusual for an employer to have a separate role for payroll administration due to the tax complexities that must be maintained according to both state and federal statutes.

Exempt vs. Non-exempt Employees

This is typically quite complex, especially for California employers and those that maintain a similar model. As of this writing, California law maintains that all employees are *not* exempt from overtime *unless* specific conditions are met. While some of those conditions do involve management and fiscal responsibilities, it is predicated on the responsibilities not the title. In other words, and by example only, it is not sufficient to provide a management title to an employee and thus consider them exempt from overtime, but rather that they actually supervise two or more subordinates. This is often a sticky area for employees and employers alike, especially as it relates to retention. While some employees and managers relish the freedom associated with an exempt role, such as the lack of necessity to maintain accurate time records, others are enticed more by the potential for overtime and the increase in personal time afforded by a non-exempt role. (*See* http://www.calchamber.com/california-employment-law/pages/exempt-nonexempt-employees.aspx)

Overtime

The potential for overtime can be quite enticing for some employees. However, overtime laws and their requisite time-keeping requirements can be challenging. As of this writing, in California, a non-exempt employee that works more than eight hours in any given day or more than forty hours in any defined work-week, is mandated to receive overtime in accordance with California employment laws. (*See* http://www.calchamber.com/california-employment-law/pages/california-overtime-pay.aspx *and see* http://www.shrm.org/templatestools/toolkits/pages/californiacomplyingwithcaliforniaovertimeandwagepaymentlaw.aspx)

Bonuses

The potential for an annual bonus can be a key to retaining key employees. However, it is not unusual for those same employees to maintain their employment only to receive such a bonus and then terminate the relationship knowing that there will not be another opportunity for another year.

The bonus structure for a commissioned sales person can also be a way to entice good people to stay motivated and keep top performers. Here's a resource for ideas on various commission compensation bonus structures: http://smallbusiness.chron.com/examples-sales-bonus-plans-15783.html

Expense Reimbursement

If handled improperly, this can be an area ripe with fraud. However, if handled properly, this can also be an area to encourage employee engagement and retention. For example: As a notary public, a California notary is required to maintain their commission in four-year increments (barring a mid-term relinquishment of their commission). However, their membership with the National Notary Association can be renewed annually or in conjunction with their commission. In one instance, a long-term employee chose the four-year membership because it was significantly cheaper than renewing annually. However, she did not confirm with her supervisor, the CFO, before renewing her membership. When the invoice arrived, the CFO was angry and felt taken advantage of by the employed notary. Even after explaining the reasoning, the CFO was visibly disturbed for many days and perhaps even weeks. Had the CFO assumed the employee's good intention rather than assuming an underhanded theft, the employed notary may have been retained by the employer longer than a few months.

Hank had a boss (who has since passed away, so he feels it is ok to add this story) who told him to pad his expense report with one type of expense to pay for another kind of expense which was not approved by corporate. This could have gotten them both in trouble.

Personal Leave

On more than one occasion, I have heard from an employee that the ability to take personal leave without evidence of retaliation has spurred loyalty for many more years than any compensation possibly could.

Breaks/Rest Periods

While these are most commonly seen with non-exempt employees who are mandated by law to take two ten-minute breaks for each eight-hour work day, the ability for an exempt employee to take a lunch or coffee break without being questioned, can also be a key to retaining their loyalty.

Appreciation

One of our friends has shared a quote with us, "Appreciation wins out over self-promotion every single time." As an unofficial non-taxable form of remuneration, show your employees how much you appreciate what they do, tell them when they are doing things the right way and when they are exceeding your expectations. Treat them to a surprise lunch, an unexpected day off, movie tickets for a show their child will like, or sponsor a softball or bowling team. There are many ways you can make your company a better place to work, a more fun place to work, and a place that your employees want to make more successful because they have done what we want all our employees to do: take ownership of a company they don't own.

Training Your Team
Types of Training
When HR talks about employment training as part of employee retention, we typically mean both teaching your organization's unique style or approach as well as professional development. Let's start with teaching your team about your organization's culture and style. Since most employees tend to like, and perform best, within a structure, human resource experts typically recommend employee training be performed as part of the regular routine. Generally, that means either quarterly, semi-annually, or annually, as well as on an as-needed basis for unique issues that may arise. Depending on the number of employees, you may want to conduct training by department, perhaps on a rotating basis so that the entire company doesn't shut down more than once a year for a company retreat. It is also generally true that what may be the perfect season for sales or marketing, may not be the perfect season for your accounting department.

You may also want to conduct employee training concurrently with training a new employee. Sometimes having a newbie in the room is a great refresher for your more seasoned employees as well as providing them a chance to shine and see how much they have learned since the last training. Since learning is a gradual process, many of us do not realize how far we have come until it is time to teach someone else and then we remember the things that we didn't know when we first started either.

Another good time for employee training is when a new rule or law that affects your industry is either on the horizon or was recently passed. For these,

I would recommend setting aside some time for an expert to come in, unless you or someone on staff is that expert.

Professional Development

As part of your employee retention efforts, it is recommended and expected that you will allow time for any necessary professional development and that you will cover the expense as well. This can be part of your benefit package and can be included in your cover letter.

Hank had it approved by his upper management that he could pay for seminars offered by their industry non-profit. If it was a seminar on a type of sales, he would invite his sales people to the event, then have them all meet for lunch afterwards to decide how the team could use what was learned that morning to their mutual benefit. The modest cost for entry plus lunch was far less expensive than if he had to bring that speaker into their company for only their employees.

Reviewing Your Team

As with most anything in life, there are pros and cons to employee reviews. Most employees expect them at least annually. Of course, most employees have a love/hate relationship with their annual review. Most of us like to know what our supervisor admires about us, and, unfortunately, we often only learn this during an annual performance review. On the other hand, most folks don't like being criticized, even in a most loving way, and thus are braced for any negative feedback they may encounter.

Supervisors, too, have a love/hate relationship with reviews. They love the bounce they get when employees know where to improve and rise to the occasion but dread the time it takes to prepare for each review, the review itself, and then any defensiveness the employee may exhibit both during the conversation as well as days and sometimes weeks after.

Here's a cautionary tale about performance reviews: If you are going to perform them, be consistent. Either perform them like clockwork for every employee (or at least every class of employee) at the same time every time (i.e. at the end of every year, at their anniversary date, or every quarter) or do *not* perform them at all. They are not required by law, but they are a best business practice.

What I meant before about "every class of employee" is this: Some employers conduct employee reviews for every employee, top to bottom. Others only do so for those that are *not* senior management, not part of the C-suite. For one employer that I worked with they would perform them for every employee, and even the senior partners would then have a partners' meeting where they would review each other. As they grew, they also formed an advisory board and then were reviewed individually and collectively by that board.

Performance reviews come in many shapes and sizes. Appendix D provides you with a sample like the one I developed for an employer. Whichever style you choose, I recommend that you use the same one for every employee before changing styles. In other words, you may find that you decide you don't like a particular style and want to change. That's fine, but only change once you have used it for each employee (i.e. for an entire round). After that, feel free to change for the next round. In this way, you avoid the appearance of bias. If you change mid-stream, you could be accused of favoritism in that you changed because you felt that someone else would do better with a different style. It may not be the case at all, but it could *appear* that way and you do not want to put yourself in the position of having to defend yourself. Better to finish a round, then announce that you will be changing the style for the following review period or season.

Policies, Procedures, and Ethics
Handbooks
I was lucky enough in my longest HR role that I entered a company that already had a handbook. It was a fun manual with only a few glitches, but it gave me a place to start. Since you are probably reading this as a small business owner, here are a few of the trickiest key points that are found in every employee handbook, or, more accurately, your policies and procedures manual.

First, I would say, that you should be creating this manual as soon as you hire your first employee. Experience has taught me that you will not make your first hiring decision lightly. Chances are you will bring someone on that you already have a relationship with in some way and already trust. If so, I would work on creating this manual together. Perhaps you will create the first draft and then finesse it with the input and assistance of your key employee. At the end of the book, in Appendix E, you'll find a resource for a templated manual which you will need to modify to match your corporate culture and your state's employment laws.

Monitoring Technology
Electronic monitoring is one of the trickiest areas, especially in our country where free speech is a staple human right. You will need to balance the

need to ensure that your employees are using the time you are paying them for wisely, as well as providing them with enough resources to get their job done with limited oversight from you, and with ample time to allow them to recharge and handle any personal needs which do arise each day, sometimes unexpectedly.

Will you be monitoring your employee's calls? Should they expect privacy? Will you be providing them with a cell phone? If so, are personal calls permitted on those devices? Or, since they probably already have one, will you be reimbursing them for company calls on their personal device? How will you compute this if they already have multiple minute prepaid plans?

Will you be monitoring your employee's email? Will you have a policy that forbids using company email for personal use? Are employees allowed time to check their personal email using the company internet connection? Are employees provided time to check their personal email or texts on their personal smart phones?

We all know how addictive internet research can be, especially social media. We also know how valuable a resource it can be. How will you monitor how much of their time is work vs. personal time? You must be very careful when it comes to personal surfing of the internet. If one employee is using your company internet to visit websites which are not *professional*, and some other employee happens to look over the shoulder of the first employee and gets offended by the content, the employer is the one who gets sued.

Ethics

It should come as no surprise that you will retain more valuable employees if your corporate ethics are impeccable, and you expect the same of your team. Clean ethics will also tend to keep you out of costly litigation. Part of clean ethics is consistent treatment of all employees, especially within their employment class. For example, it is one thing to have policies for exempt employees, and different policies for non-exempt employees, but it is quite different to have different policies within those classes and even more of an issue for those that hold the same title.

Safety First
Emergency Drills

Too many employers dismiss this as not relevant and not important. And it may not be *the* top priority, but in an emergency it suddenly becomes the *only* priority so make the time to show your employees exactly how valuable they are by helping everyone prepare for an emergency. And do not forget about your employees' families either. Help your employees prepare their families for an emergency so that they can focus on the workplace, knowing that they have prepared their families and have a plan where to meet them when they can. There are many resources for emergency preparedness. My favorite in the Los Angeles area, and online, is SOS (http://www.sosproducts.com). The Red Cross also puts out great check lists (http://www.redcross.org/get-help/prepare-for-emergencies/be-red-cross-ready). If you are in leased office space, your property manager probably conducts regular drills, typically annually or semi-annually.

Most local fire departments host events where this topic is covered in depth.

First Aid

Such a simple thing as having a consistently stocked and readily available first aid kit that employees can access when they have minor injuries such as paper cuts, staple issues, etc., as well as more serious needs when waiting for emergency personnel to arrive, demonstrate to them that their well-being is important to you. Ready-made kits and replacement supplies can be purchased from SOS Products and the Red Cross as well as from your local office supply stores.

Holidays

Many employers think that holiday parties need to be big, elaborate events. However, I submit to you that even small, pot-luck events demonstrate to your employees that you recognize that there is more to life than work and that the relationships forged under your employ do indeed matter and thus should be celebrated. By the way, please do not forget the other holidays that show up periodically throughout the year such as the company's birthday and each employee birthday. Just as each employee should receive a welcome card from HR, their hiring manager and the company's founder/CEO/COO/president (whatever the right title is in your organization), they should also receive a card on their birthday. There are many services that allow you to do this affordably and from the comfort of your office. My favorite is still www.IDeserveItAll.com which can be customized to the individual employee and can be mailed either to their home, or to the office, whichever makes the most sense for your corporate culture (or done from your smartphone at www.YuloffCreative.com/cards).

Succession Planning

Since no one I know ever plans on staying in the same role for their entire career, I encourage every employee (yes, even those at the very top) to think of what their successor will need to know to be successful in their role. One way to do this relatively easily is to take the time to document every task as if someone had to come in cold (in the unlikely event the employee awoke with amnesia one day and forgot they were supposed to come to work) to do their job, even if only for a day. This means documenting what you do every moment of every day, as well as how you do it, with screenshots whenever possible. These documents should be revisited regularly (I advise monthly or quarterly, depending on the role and the corporate culture) since roles and procedures can change and thus the documents may need to be revised.

The very first book Hank wrote was as a senior in college. The advertising department for the newspaper for which he was the manager had faster turn-over than the editorial department and he found that each year, the processes had to be re-learned by his department. He spent quite a bit of time his last semester creating a process book—or succession plan—for the following advertising managers.

Chapter 5

Voting Your Weakest Link Off the Island— Terminations

Although most employees are *at will*, given our litigious society, it is not in your best interest to simply wake up one morning and decide to terminate an employee unless there is some provable, egregious wrong perpetrated, like theft or violence. In most circumstances it is better to set up your case as if it were going to go to court. This means document, document, document!

Preparation and Set Up

Termination is a process *not* an event: A termination need not follow a three-strikes rule. Some offenses are so egregious that only the one strike is sufficient to terminate, such as theft or assault, to name only two.

Disciplinary Actions

I'll bet you know that the three most important words in real estate are "Location, location, location." Well, the three most important words in HR are "documentation, documentation, documentation." Whenever an employee needs to be disciplined, be sure to document. The most effective documentation is a memo, memorializing the conversation that both you and the employee sign before placing the document in the employee's personnel file. It is advisable to provide a sample of the template form in the Employee Handbook. See Appendix E for one such example.

Termination Notices

Each termination should be accompanied by a termination notice. Perhaps it goes without saying, but since you do not want to find yourself in a "he said, she said" scenario it is advisable to document the reason (if any) as well as the date of the termination and any other agreements that were made between the employer and the employee at the time of termination. Part of such notice should include what employment materials must remain behind such as computers, keys, passkeys, clients lists, etc. Sometimes that notice includes a severance package. Sample termination notices and agreements are found in Appendix E.

Exit Interviews

This is the official name of the conversation between human resources and the terminated employee, regardless of the reason. Part of this conversation is to review the termination agreement, advising the employee of their rights, finding out if there are any outstanding workers compensation issues or any other grievances that may not have yet been divulged, and collect the employer's assets that may still remain in the employee's possession. These conversations should take place even when the employee has chosen to terminate the relationship. A sample exit interview document is found in Appendix E.

Escorting off the Premises

As uncomfortable as it is for both parties, it is considered good business practice for someone to escort the employee off the premises. If there is concern of violence or retaliation, ask a security officer to escort the terminated employee to their car and/or off the premises. However, if the only concern is that appropriate materials are not removed, then someone from HR or another member of the senior management team can perform this function. It is rarely advisable that the employee's direct supervisor ever escort the terminated employee. It is too easy for the employee to attempt to renegotiate the terms of their termination or to create a scenario where new allegations can be made. If the separation is relatively amicable and yet the employee is emotional, it may be of benefit to offer a friendly employee take a few minutes to walk out with the terminated employee to offer emotional support and maybe even a friendly hug. Since employees often spend many hours together, it should not be a surprise that some employees form long lasting friendships with their colleagues. Saying goodbye to these friends that they will no longer see every day can be the hardest part of separating from an employer.

Mitigating the Risk of a Lawsuit

Although we touched on litigation before, there are two areas that require special attention as it relates to termination.

Separation Agreements

A separation agreement is the legal document that delineates both the employee's and employer's rights, as well as what assets must remain with the employer and what the employee may take off site. These agreements are reviewed with the employee as part of the exit interview. Sample agreements have been provided as part of Appendix E.

Severance Packages
Sometimes it is advantageous to provide monetary remuneration to a terminated employee. Perhaps the termination is really a lay off and thus a week or more of severance pay is offered to help mitigate the unexpected termination. Or, perhaps, there were one or more agreements executed either upon initial employment and/or during employment that afforded the employee some set amounts due upon termination. Sample documentation is attached as Appendix E.

Even After They're Gone
Yes, I know you thought your responsibilities to your employees ended when they left your employ. Unfortunately, that may not be the case.

COBRA
If you provide health insurance to your employees, your terminated employees are entitled to COBRA coverage. According to the US Department of Labor (https://www.dol.gov/agencies/ebsa/about-ebsa/our-activities/resource-center/faqs/cobra-continuation-health-coverage-compliance), "Congress passed the landmark Consolidated Omnibus Budget Reconciliation Act health benefit provisions in 1986. The law amends the Employee Retirement Income Security Act, the Internal Revenue Code and the Public Health Service Act to provide continuation of group health coverage that otherwise might be terminated."

That only sort of helps you, "COBRA contains provisions giving certain former employees, retirees, spouses former spouses, and dependent children the right to temporary continuation of health coverage at group rates. This coverage, however, is only available when coverage is lost due to certain specific events. Group health coverage for COBRA participants is usually more expensive than health coverage for active employees, since usually the employer pays a part of the premium for active employees while COBRA participants generally pay the entire premium themselves. It is ordinarily less expensive, though, than individual health coverage."

Want some good news? "Employers with twenty or more employees are usually required to offer COBRA coverage and to notify their employees of the availability of such coverage. COBRA applies to plans maintained by private-sector employers and sponsored by most state and local governments." I'm guessing, if you are reading this book, you do not have twenty employees, so you have a ways to go before this impacts you, but you need to know so that you can plan ahead accordingly.

Unemployment
In some instances, terminated employees may be entitled to unemployment benefits. For information on eligibility requirements, we return to the US Department of Labor: https://www.dol.gov/general/topic/unemployment-insurance

Workers' Compensation
According to current California law, employees who are injured on the job must immediately file a claim. However, sometimes employees are unaware that their injury could be related to their employment until after their employment ends and they find that they have the time to explore the cause of their injury with their health care provider. As of this writing, regardless of the separation agreement, a terminated employee cannot sign away their rights to Workers' Compensation.

What If They Are Not on Site
For many companies there are employees who are not in the same office—for example, outside sales representatives who are in different states. You need to follow the same rules, as closely as possible. Especially if they have property which belongs to the company including sales records, training manuals, and office equipment.

Chapter 6

But It's the Law

One of the most important functions of the human resource role is to be sure that everyone in the company complies with all regulations that apply to them. In this chapter we're going to talk about protecting the organization and its employees, and we'll cover the major federal legislation that affects most companies. This is not legal advice and you should always consult your own employment law attorney or PEO for guidance as to your specific situation and decisions.

And as many small businesses have an HR department of one, we'll talk about the challenges, minimum requirements, and best practices for a department of one.

Keeping Out of Trouble—-Risk Mitigation

There are some laws that employers may find intrusive and thus will try to ignore, hoping that their employees either don't know about them or are so grateful for the employment opportunity that they will not report an infraction to the appropriate authority. Any HR professional will encourage the employer against taking such a risk. Mitigating risk is a key function of the human resources department. Here are the most common laws that employers tend to ignore.

Diversity

As you are probably aware, people discriminate all the time. Although it is unkind, it is often not illegal. However, when it comes to employment law, there are instances in which you may *not* discriminate without breaking a law.

Federal law prohibits discrimination on the basis of race, gender, pregnancy, national origin (including affiliation with a Native American tribe),

31

religion, disability, citizenship status, genetic information, and age (if the person is at least forty years old).

State and local laws often prohibit additional types of discrimination, including discrimination on the basis of marriage, sexual orientation, and weight. Almost half of the states prohibit private employers from making employment decisions based on sexual orientation, as do many county and municipal governments. To learn more about your state and local laws, contact your state fair employment office.

Emergency Preparedness

This is one of those issues that should be handled by human resources in conjunction with the office manager. Since the office manager is typically the one in charge of purchasing office products and supplies, HR may need to advise on what specific supplies needed, how often they should be replenished, and how and when they should be used. Policies should include when it is advisable to shelter in place versus evacuate. In addition to it being a legal requirement in multi-story buildings, it is also highly advisable, and a good HR move, to provide a feeling of safety and comfort for your employees. You may want to ensure that each employee also has an emergency preparedness plan in place at home, as well appropriate supplies. If employees know that their families are safe, then they can better focus on their workplace.

Employment Practices Liability Insurance (EPLI)

In order to protect the business from job-related lawsuits and claims, business owners should consider a type of insurance known as employment practices liability insurance, or EPLI. An EPLI policy offers protection against claims and lawsuits that are brought against a business, its officers or directors, or its employees and managers. These policies generally cover charges in the following areas governed by the Family Medical Leave Act and the Americans with Disabilities Act: gender, age, and other types of discrimination, sexual harassment, wrongful termination or discipline, negligent decisions (such as compensation, promotion, or hiring), breach of contract for employment, emotional distress or mental anguish, invasion of privacy, libel or slander, or employee benefits mismanagement.

While some insurance policies for the company's directors and officers may contain employment practices liability insurance coverage, the coverage is usually limited to directors and officers, and may have greater exclusions than a standalone EPLI policy. Personnel policies should be the first line of defense against employment-related claims.

The cost of EPLI coverage will vary based on the type, size, and risk profile of your business. The insurance company may want to see your written personnel policies to help them determine the risk and cost of your policy. The cost of legal defense is typically included in the aggregate insurance limits, along with the costs of judgments and settlements. Criminal conduct is not generally covered by EPLI.

First Aid

Much like emergency preparedness, this is another of those items that could be handled by both human resources and/or the office manager. It is such an important item, that I think it is better to have two people share the responsibility. First-aid kits can be purchased from most office supply stores, as well as other locations, both on- and off-line. I also recommend that every human resource executive be trained in first aid and recertified on a predetermined regular basis. For the really dedicated, I also recommend CERT certification. The Community Emergency Response Team (CERT) Program educates people about disaster preparedness for hazards that may impact their area and trains them in basic disaster response skills, such as fire safety, light search and rescue, team organization, and disaster medical operations. The Red Cross also holds disaster training, which I recommend to every dedicated HR professional.

Notices and Postings

There are certain notices that must be posted in an area that is accessible and frequented by both employees and applicants. According to the U.S. Department of Labor, posting requirements vary by statute, and not all employers are covered by each of the department's statutes and therefore they may not be required to post a specific notice. For example, some small businesses may not be covered by the Family and Medical Leave Act and thus would not be subject to the act's posting requirements.

The elaws Poster Advisor site can be used to determine which posters employers are required to display at their place of business. Posters may be downloaded free of charge and printed directly from the site. For information on state poster requirements visit the appropriate state departments of labor.

Discrimination

There are several major pieces of legislation that address discrimination in the work place. The following are the most notable.

Americans with Disabilities Act of 1990 (ADA)/ Rehabilitation Act of 1973: The ADA prohibits employers from discriminating against people with disabilities (including mental illness) in any aspect of employment, including applications, interviews, testing, hiring, job assignments, evaluations, compensation, leave, benefits, discipline, training, promotions, medical exams, layoffs, and firing.

Age Discrimination in Employment Act (ADEA): The act prohibits discrimination based on age against employees who are at least forty years old. Prohibited activities include discrimination on the basis of age in hiring, promotion, discharge, compensation, or terms, conditions or privileges of employment. It also prohibits employers from retaliating against an applicant or employee for asserting his or her rights under the ADEA.

Title VII of the Civil Rights Act of 1964: This is specifically aimed at employment discrimination. It prohibits employers who have fifteen or more employees each working day from discriminating against applicants and employees on the basis of race, color, religion, sex, and national origin (including membership in a Native American tribe). It was amended again in 1978 to prohibit discrimination on the basis of pregnancy as well. It also prohibits harassment in the workplace based on membership in a protected class, for example gender identity.

The Equal Pay Act (EPA): This act mandates that employers must give men and women the same pay if they perform the same work. While the work does not have to be identical, it must be substantially similar. That is, if men and women perform jobs that require the same skills, effort, and responsibility under similar working conditions, they are performing the same work. Employers may not give male and female employees different wages based on sex, but may discriminate on the basis of (i) a seniority system; (ii) a merit system; (iii) a system which measures earnings by quantity or quality of production; or (iv) a differential based on any other factor other than sex.

Genetic Information Nondiscrimination Act (GINA): This 2008 law prohibits private employers (as well as people insured through Medicare) from using an applicant's or employee's genetic information as the basis for employment decisions and requires employers to keep genetic information confidential. It also prohibits group health plans and health insurers from denying coverage to a healthy individual or charging that person higher premiums based solely on a genetic predisposition to developing a disease in the future. However, the law does not cover life, disability, or long-term care insurance, which may cause some reluctance to get tested.

The Immigration Reform and Control Act of 1986 (IRCA): This act makes it illegal for an employer to discriminate with respect to any aspect of employment (including hiring, firing, pay, job assignments, promotions, layoff, training, fringe benefits, and any other term or condition of employment), based upon an individual's citizenship or immigration status. National origin discrimination involves treating people (applicants or employees) unfavorably because they are from a particular country or part of the world, because of ethnicity or accent, because they are married to (or associated with) a person of a certain national origin, or because they appear to be of a certain ethnic background (even if they are not). The law also prohibits employers from hiring only U.S. citizens or lawful permanent residents unless required to do so by law, regulation or government contract

The Omnibus Crime Control and Safe Streets Act of 1968 (and similar laws affecting law enforcement): This prohibits employment discrimination on the basis of race, color, national origin, religion, or sex, in OJP (Office of Justice Programs), OVW (Office on Violence Against Women), and COPS (Office of Community Oriented Policing Services) funded programs or activities.

Harassment

The main thing to remember about harassment is that it is defined by the *victim*. If there is something you said or did to me that I find objectionable and I advised you of such and you continue to do it, then it is considered *harassment*. According to the EEOC, Harassment is a form of discrimination. Although the news tends to highlight the titillating details of sexual harassment, it is by no means the only form. Harassment is unwelcome conduct that is based on race, color, religion, sex (including pregnancy), national origin, age (forty or older), disability or genetic information. Harassment becomes unlawful where 1) enduring the offensive conduct becomes a condition of continued employment, or 2) the conduct is severe or pervasive enough to create a work environment that a reasonable person would consider intimidating, hostile, or abusive.

Anti-discrimination laws also prohibit harassment against individuals in retaliation for filing a discrimination charge, testifying, or participating in any way in an investigation, proceeding, or lawsuit under these laws; or opposing employment practices that they reasonably believe discriminate against individuals, in violation of these laws. Petty slights, annoyances, and isolated incidents (unless extremely serious) will not rise to the level of illegality. To be unlawful, the conduct must create a work environment that would be intimidating, hostile, or offensive to reasonable people. Offensive conduct may include, but is not limited to, offensive jokes, slurs, epithets or name calling, physical assaults or threats, intimidation, ridicule or mockery, insults or put-downs, offensive objects or pictures, and interference with work performance.

Harassment can occur in a variety of circumstances, including, but not limited to, the following:

- The harasser can be the victim's supervisor, a supervisor in another area, an agent of the employer, a co-worker, or a non-employee.
- The victim does not have to be the person harassed but can be anyone affected by the offensive conduct.
- Unlawful harassment may occur without economic injury to, or discharge of, the victim. Prevention is the best tool to eliminate harassment in the workplace.

Employers are encouraged to take appropriate steps to prevent and correct unlawful harassment. They should clearly communicate to employees that unwelcome harassing conduct will not be tolerated. They can do this by establishing an effective complaint or grievance process, providing anti-harassment training to their managers and employees, and taking immediate and appropriate action when an employee complains. Employers should strive to create an environment in which employees feel free to raise concerns and are confident that those concerns will be addressed.

The employer should encourage employees to inform the harasser directly that the conduct is unwelcome and must stop. Tell them to report harassment to management at an early stage to prevent its escalation.

The employer is automatically liable for harassment by a supervisor that results in a negative employment action such as termination, failure to promote or hire, and loss of wages. If the supervisor's harassment results in a hostile work environment, the employer can avoid liability only if it can prove that: 1) it reasonably tried to prevent and promptly correct the harassing behavior; and 2) the employee unreasonably failed to take advantage of any preventive or corrective opportunities provided by the employer.

The employer will be liable for harassment by non-supervisory employees or non-employees over whom it has control (e.g., independent contractors or customers on the premises), if it knew, or should have known about the harassment and failed to take prompt and appropriate corrective action.

The Health Information Patient Protection Act (HIPPA)
This is a very important piece of the benefits administrator role. In a small business, this is often the person that handles other HR duties, which can put this person in an important and sometimes conflicted role. The benefits

administrator may learn of an employee's health issue, before the employee is ready to disclose said issue to the employer, or the immediate supervisor. This person must advise and encourage the employee to disclose on their own. Once the employer is advised, the employer/supervisor is now also bound by the same HIPPA law and is forbidden from sharing the specifics with anyone unless they receive written authorization from the employee, or the employee makes their health issue known publicly on their own. (See Appendix H for more information.)

The Fair Labor Standards Act (FLSA)
There are many parts to this law. Here are some major areas.

- Child Labor: These provisions are designed to protect the educational opportunities of minors and prohibit their employment in jobs and under conditions detrimental to their health or well-being.

- Exempt or non-exempt: This is an issue that trips up many employers and can cost them heftily if they are found to have not administered it perfectly, especially according to today's California laws (which is why you'll find this topic discussed multiple times throughout this publication). According to California, all employees are seen as non-exempt, unless they meet some specific exceptions. Those exceptions fall into very specific categories, namely administrative, budgetary, discretionary, and management. As common as these terms may appear, their specific definitions as they relate to FLSA must be conscientiously reviewed before any employee is classified as exempt from overtime laws. Appendix F provides a listing of recommended places to review the current FLSA rules.

- Legal definition of hours worked: Hours worked ordinarily include all the time during which an employee is required to be on the employer's premises, on duty, or at a prescribed workplace. Yes, even if your employees telecommute, you still need to be mindful of their hours worked.

- Minimum wage: The federal minimum wage is set by the federal government, but many states also have minimum wage laws which pay a higher rate. In cases where an employee is subject to both state and federal minimum wage laws, the employee is entitled to the higher minimum wage.

- Overtime: This part of the law can get quite complex and many employers have lost millions of dollars when an employee (or employees in a class action law suit) file for past overtime pay due to them. Covered nonexempt employees must receive overtime pay for hours worked over forty hours per workweek (any fixed and regularly recurring period of 168 hours — seven consecutive 24-hour periods) at a rate not less than one and one-half times the regular rate of pay. There is no limit on the number of hours employees sixteen years or older may work in any workweek. The employer is not required to pay overtime for work on weekends, holidays, or regular days of rest, unless overtime is worked on such days.

- Recordkeeping requirements: Employers must display an official poster outlining the requirements of the Fair Labor Standards Act. Employers must also keep employee time and pay records.

The Family Medical Leave Act (FMLA): This act includes all family medical leave issues, such as ailing parents, spouses, and children as well as pregnancy leave. It provides certain employees with up to twelve weeks of unpaid, job-protected leave per year. It also requires that their group health benefits be maintained during the leave.

Employee or Consultant (W2 vs 1099)
As you are considering your first employee(s), it is often tempting to contract with independent consultants. However, if you are requiring them to perform their duties during set hours and/or in particular ways using your tools (however that is defined for your industry), they are legally considered employees and must be classified as such as per IRS Rules. (See Appendix H).

Mileage Allowance
If you are a small business, chances are employees often run employment-related errands using their own vehicle, for which they are entitled to compensation. That compensation is defined by the IRS. The mileage allowance allocation to which such an employee is entitled (in addition to their compensation) is calculated to cover their gas and care of their vehicle. (Refer to the current IRS amount.) It is recommended that you require employees to record their starting and ending odometer readings (contemporaneous log), which may be provided by a photo, and submitted as part of their standard expense reimbursement report (samples are in Appendix G).

Minimum Wage
The minimum wage is being hotly contested both nationally and locally. As its name describes, it is the lowest wage an employer is legally mandated to

pay an employee. If you employ professionals, this may not be an issue for you except for maybe your most entry level employees.

The National Labor Relations Act (NLRA)

This 1935 law was enacted to protect the rights of employees and employers, to encourage collective bargaining, and to curtail certain private sector labor and management practices, which could harm the general welfare of workers, businesses and the U.S. economy.

I haven't had a lot of experience with this law since I only worked for one employer who dealt with this issue and was concerned about employees unionizing. As the HR director, it was one of my core duties to ensure that the we did all we could to make sure that the employees didn't unionize. Although the company was very concerned about the potential issue, they continued treating their employees terribly and provided little guidance for their improvement so that they could progress in their careers. Although my role ended when my employer was acquired by a multi-national corporation, as far as I know, the employees never did unionize. My only other experience with unions is second hand. My father-in-law helped create the first pharmacists' union and my stepmother helped to form a local nurses chapter at the hospital where she worked.

The Occupational Safety and Health Act (OSHA)

This is another of those laws that many business owners with professional employees tend to ignore, erroneously thinking that it only applies to trade employees. Here are some of the most ubiquitous aspects for all businesses.

Ergonomics. Repetitive stress injuries exacerbated by poor ergonomics are probably the most hazardous issue for your standard office worker, and OSHA is paying close attention, as should you. As you create your own and your employees' work stations, it is advisable that you review and follow the ergonomic guidelines provided by OSHA (see Appendix F). There are professionals that specialize in reviewing your ergonomics. The one I know the best is Joshua Dunn of www.NotCarpalTunnel.com.

Hazards. Part of HR's role is that of risk mitigation. Being mindful of office hazards is typically the role of the office manager, but in a small office where there is not an office manager, HR typically fills this role as well. One of the hazards we need to be most mindful of in California is earthquakes. Therefore, it is important to ensure that nothing is left unsecured on a high shelf, especially above an employee. Another hazard to be mindful of is a fire. As such, according to current Los Angeles building code rules, there must be at least an eighteen-inch clearance from the ceiling (nothing may be placed so high as to intrude upon that eighteen-inch cushion).

Health and Safety. An OSHA safety plan is a written document that describes the process for identifying the physical and health hazards that could harm workers. It should include procedures to prevent accidents, and the steps to take when accidents occur. It is the blueprint for keeping workers safe. This plan is often compiled into a single safety manual.

I highly recommend the BLR site and programs (http://www.blr.com/safetytips/safety-plans), which I referred to regularly while HR manager at a financial services firm.

BLR has over seventy customizable prewritten safety program templates and more than one hundred associated forms as well as practical compliance analysis. Their safety plans, forms, and training resources are available in several timesaving formats. Their knowledgeable editors continually add new OSHA safety plan topics. If you need a safety compliance solution, BLR probably has it.

Violence in the workplace. With an increase in incidents of domestic violence, there is also an increase in the incidents of violence in the workplace. As such, it is imperative that your HR personnel be open, accessible and receptive to any employee's claim of domestic violence and prepare the front office staff for intrusion by the abusive partner. For more information on workplace violence, please see OSHA's dedicated site at https://www.osha.gov/SLTC/workplaceviolence.

Privacy Laws
Federal, state, and local legislation provide a basic source of protection against invasion of privacy by private parties, including employers. Legislation also limits privacy rights, however, that may otherwise exist under common law or other statutes. The law on privacy varies greatly from state to state and it is important to know the laws for your state. You can find information on these laws on the BLR site as well. Some of the important topics they cover are:
- Privacy in the Pre-Employment Process
- Privacy in the Workplace
- Workplace Surveillance
- Personnel Records
- Employers' Private Information

The Uniformed Services Employment and Reemployment Rights Act of 1994 (USERRA)

This is a federal law that establishes rights and responsibilities for uniformed service members and their civilian employers. Since employers are required to provide information about these rights to those entitled to those rights and benefits under USERRA, a notice of those rights, benefits and obligations is typically part of the notice postings that must be maintained where employee notices are customarily placed, and is entitled, "Your Rights under USERRA."

Visas

The Department of State says that,

> Generally, a citizen of a foreign country who wishes to enter the United States must first obtain a visa, either a nonimmigrant visa for temporary stay, or an immigrant visa for permanent residence. Temporary worker visas are for persons who want to enter the United States for employment lasting a fixed period of time and are not considered permanent or indefinite. Each of these visas requires the prospective employer to first file a petition with U.S. Citizenship and Immigration Services (USCIS). An approved petition is required to apply for a work visa.

Temporary workers must qualify for the available visa category based on the planned employment purpose. The steps in the process before applying for a visa vary. Review the employment groupings and categories on the Department of State site: http://travel.state.gov/content/visas/english/employment.html.

This was not an issue for most of my days as head of HR departments, so my personal experience is limited. While working for an independent distribution company, the owners had family members in a different country that they occasionally (twice that I recall) wanted to employ. I remember needing to place an ad to make it seem as if we were looking for employees everywhere and the best qualified was this one person in the country where their family member lived.

My next two employers didn't want the hassle or the expense of the legal process necessary to obtain a work visa for foreign nationals unless that applicant was so motivated that they were willing to do all the work and pay all of the expense.

However, my last employer was a multinational company and thus had a whole department devoted to obtaining the appropriate work visas. Nonetheless, that was a few years ago and I seem to remember that these rules change rather frequently. For the most up to date rules, regulations, forms and information, I recommend you visit the U.S. Department of State.

A Special Case—California Laws

My experience has been with California law and, typically, though not always, if you go by California law, since it is such an employee-friendly state, you are in good or better standing than if you use any other state's laws.

At Will

This one always confused my employers because it is not a blanket law—there are loads of exceptions. According to the California Labor Code, California is an at-will employment state. Under the at-will presumption, a California employer, absent an agreement or statutory or public policy exception to the contrary, may terminate an employee for any reason at any time (and an employee can resign for any reason at any time, though a two-week notice is customary). Statutory exceptions include terminating an employee for reasons based on discrimination laws, for participating in union activity, or for refusing to carry out an activity that violates the law. To reduce exposure to wrongful discharge liability, use at-will language in all written and verbal communications with employees—job announcements, interviews, employee handbooks, training seminars, and employee reviews. Do not use language that indicates job security or permanence. Additional information and guidelines on at-will employment and other labor management issues can be found by consulting your state's labor site or the California Labor Law Digest, California Chamber of Commerce, or the State of California website for business (see Appendix H for the links to these sites.)

Jury Duty

When employers are given reasonable advance notice, employees are entitled to take time off to serve as a juror or as a witness if subpoenaed to appear at trial. The employer is not required to pay non-exempt employees for time not worked due to jury service. However, an employer may choose to compensate their employees for a period of time. Employers should have a jury duty policy that is consistent with other policies for taking time off due to non-personal, non-voluntary reasons, and it should be uniformly enforced. In the case of an exempt employee, the employer must continue to pay the full weekly salary unless the jury service prevents the exempt employee from performing any work for a full week.

If your circles are like ours, having to enforce a jury duty policy was generally irrelevant because everyone worked hard to get out of jury duty. I always thought it might be fun to sit on a jury, but somehow those notices always arrive at the wrong time. There was once when I was not successful and wound up being an alternate. That means having to sit through all the testimony, coming up with my own opinion on the verdict, but not being able to share it with anyone!

Chapter 7

Your HR Department

A Department of One

Most of my career I spent as a department of one, just me. There were a few months when I had the pleasure of a dedicated assistant, and there were times when my assistant was also the receptionist so she (in my case it was always a *she*) was shared with the rest of the office (not dedicated to me).

My first step when taking over a department (which included starting a department from a solo-preneur who was also handling HR duties without knowledge of best practices) was to perform an HR audit.

An HR Audit

The purpose of an HR audit it to take an objective look at the company's human resource policies, practices, procedures, and strategies. And then by using best practices, revise them to protect the company, and identify opportunities for improvement. The results can aid decision-makers focus on what areas need improvement. The Society for Human Resource Management is an excellent resource for this (see Appendix H).

HR audits typically review legal compliance, best practices, alignment with the business strategy, and HR functions (such as payroll, performance management, records retention, etc.)

The most common error found during an initial HR audit is a violation of the wage and hour laws.

The Wage and Hour Investigation

A solo-preneur's most frequent first hire is a friend or consultant whose duties morph into a role that should be correctly classified as an employee. Although the IRS guidelines are quite specific, the basics are that as an employee it is the employer that sets the hours, provides the tools and sets the parameters for how a project must be completed.

In contrast, when a role is appropriately filled by a consultant, it is they who set their own hours, use their own tools and accomplish the project for which they were hired in whatever manner they deem best to get the task completed.

The best checklist I found to prepare for a formal Department of Labor audit—and to conduct your own—is provided by an employment law firm—Lexology. (You can find a link to their site in Appendix H.)

HR Minimum Requirements

Many companies have a single person managing all the human resource functions. That makes it critical that it be the *right* person.

The minimum requirements for an HR Department of one are:
- Good organizational skills
- Good relationship skills
- Ability to move quickly and easily from one task to another
- Ability to impartially mediate between two or more parties
- Ability and interest in keeping abreast of ever changing employment laws
- Creating and maintaining an employee manual

For additional resources on managing an HR department of one see Appendix H.

HR Metrics

This is the best way to measure if your HR efforts are paying off for you. For most small businesses, I would recommend the following items to track and measure:
- HR cost per employee
- HR cost vs revenue
- Legal costs related to HR
- Settlement costs and penalties (as they relate to HR issues)
- Cost per hire
- Hiring cycle time (How long from when you wanted to hire until the new employee's start date.)
- Voluntary termination rate within the first year (How many new hires make it past the first year? If this is high, you have a problem that needs to be addressed.)
- Involuntary Termination Rate Within the First Year (How many are fired within the first year? Again, if this is high, you have a problem

that needs to be addressed.)
- Average days absent
- Average cost to terminate
- Cost of benefits as a percentage of salary
- Cost of benefits as a percentage of revenue
- Training costs per employee

Record Keeping

In real estate, the mantra is always location, location, location. In HR, the mantra is document, document, document—if you don't document it, it didn't happen. (I know I said this before, but it's *really* important.) We are taught to think of it this way: If you can't prove it in a court of law, then it is a matter of, "He said, she said," so document it and file the note in the correct folder so that you can at least prove your side in the argument. Make sure it is time stamped and include your rational for whatever decision, policy, etc. that you are making.

Administrative or Strategic

Most employers see the HR role as strictly administrative—checking the boxes on hiring, disciplining, etc. However, with the right person in that role, this can be quite the strategic partnership. This means that you include your HR professional in all business strategy sessions so that the human capital repercussions can be included in the discussion. For example, if you are planning on making a business shift, what changes need to be made to your workforce? Do you have the right people in place to make the necessary changes, or do you need to terminate some positions to make room for new ones? These are conversations that many business owners neglect to have unless their HR professional is included at the table.

Chapter 8

One Special Focus for Your Business— Think Sales

Finding the Right Salesperson for Your Business

When people ask me, "Hank, how do I find the right salesperson?" I know that it is going to be quite a conversation. Commission sales has been my primary occupation since I was in college. Even though our company has evolved into more of a service business where we provide business coaching that is focused on teaching you to create your marketing path, build your team, and get more business, I still hold true to the mantra that no matter what you and I do for a living we are all in sales. Your receptionist is the first salesperson a potential client speaks to, so he better understands what you do and how you do it, and how to promote the company.

Here are the first ten questions I am going to ask when I want to find the right salesperson. This first section takes about twenty minutes maximum and gives me the outline of the prospect as a salesperson. If the answers are great, we will move on to the more creative section. You can even ask these questions in a phone pre-interview prior to meeting face-to-face.

- What does sales mean to you? *(Let's see what they think of being in a sales environment.)*
- What made you decide to get into sales? *(Instead of that "tell me about yourself" question.)*
- What interested you about our company? Why do you want to sell for us? *(I want to see what research they did into our company.* Important note here: *if at any time a salesperson prospect uses the phrase, "Sales is sales, it does not matter what I am selling," then this is the wrong person. He will be job hopping, chasing each bright shiny object.)*
- What was your average sale in previous jobs? *(If your product costs $9997 and they are used to selling $500 products, this is going to be a huge jump in asking for the sale.)*

49

- What has been the length of your average sales cycle? *(Let's see how long she had to follow up on sales.)*
- What do you think of sales quotas? How do you use them to motivate yourself?
- How do you prospect? *(I want to see what kind of sales tools she uses.)*
- What is your last sales manager going to tell me about you when I call?
- Do you consider sales a career? *(Ninety percent will say, "Yes," which allows you to ask the next question.)*
- How do you improve yourself as a sales person? *(Let's see what kind of continuing education they are getting.)*

By now, I am going to know if I like the person sitting in front of me for the job that we have open. Those first ten questions will give me an idea if I want to continue. If not, do your best wrap up it up. But, if you are interested in this person, move forward with the following questions.

- Tell me about your best sale ever. Then ask these follow up questions:
  * Where did the lead come from?
  * What was your first step towards the sale?
  * How did you feel when they said, *"Yes?"*
  * How did you follow up after the sale?
  * Did you ask for referrals from them?
- Is that your most creative sale ever? *(Let's see if he wants to tell me about past sales. A great salesperson will have a lot of these stories.)*
- Did you ever make a sale and wish you hadn't made it? *(Here, I'm searching for honesty; allowing them to think about their past. They will likely never have heard this question, unless it was from someone else who read this book.)*
- How did your previous company obtain sales leads?
- If I asked to look at your calendar while you sold for another company, what would I see? *(This question goes along with my theory that if most salespeople were arrested and charged with being a salesperson, there would not be enough evidence to convict them. A calendar that is mostly blank will make the viewer snow blind because there is so much white paper without anything on it—there is not enough planned activity. Of course, some sales positions have internal technology that manages follow up. What I want to know is how does this person manage their sales process, or are they just catching sales on the fly and moving on.)*
- What percentage of your presentations turned into sales? *(This is going to vary by industry. Anywhere between twenty and eighty percent*

is normal for most industries. What I am looking for here is, do they know their numbers and how do they present them to you.)

- In six months, what about you is going to tell me, "Wow I am so glad I hired _____?" *(Let's see if she plans on being with us that long and if she has a plan for success.)*
- What kind of customer relationship tracking system did you use at past jobs?
- How do you define success?

The last few questions are to throw them off guard just a bit and see how they think on their feet.

- Do you think this interview has been a success? *(The standard answer will be, "It depends, are you hiring me?" Your answer is the next question.)*
- How are you going to close me?
- Do you have any questions for me? What have I forgotten to ask you?

The final question will let you know for sure if this is the right person.

- How are you going to follow up with this interview? (This question will probably throw her off guard. You are looking for something more than the standard thank-you email. I want to see if they have a bit of a sense of humor as well. "I am thinking of sending you flowers, so I will need to know how your favorite bouquet is composed." The best answer would be for them to mention two or three different methods of connecting with you—email, handwritten note, phone call, connect on a social media platform. This shows that they are used to doing the same thing with a prospect.

Finding the right salesperson is not an easy process. They don't do what you do, but they have to be able to sell what you do. For example, if you hire a salesperson to bring business into your law or dental practice, they are not a lawyer or dentist. If you hire them to bring business into your auto body shop, they are not technicians who fix car bodies. You are hiring someone who is going to have to tell your story in an interesting way and make someone know, love, and trust you. They are going to have to understand that the average sale takes between five and twelve touches. They are going to have to put up with people saying, "No," and "I need more information," without feeling let down.

You can make your job easier by making the ads you run as clear as possible as to what the salesperson is going to be selling and what they are going to be doing to sell your product. You can give them an honest idea of the range of income that they can reach, and the amount of time it will take them to get there. A well-written ad will make your entire process easier.

If you need assistance in learning how to interview sales people, head to www.FreeHRConsultation.com. We will go over how you advertise and interview your new team members.

Teaching Proper Phone Etiquette—How You Lost the Sale Before You Had a Chance to Make It

We have all experienced *phone hell*. It happens when a business has not trained their receptionist, other employees, or the virtual assistant in the proper phone etiquette for that company. We enter phone hell when proper phone etiquette is not followed. One of a few things may happen in your company that will send your potential customer into hell and lose the sale before it begins:

- The phone is *never* answered by a live person.
- The phone is answered by an answering machine that says, "Our options have changed, to please listen to all of them . . ." at which point your customer just starts pounding the *zero key* over and over hoping to be transferred to an operator.
- The phone is answered by voice mail that is a machine voice.
- Once you are transferred to an operator, he speaks too loudly, too softly, is unintelligible, or too fast to understand what he is saying.
- He transfers the call to the wrong department.
- He hangs up before the transfer goes through, leaving the potential customer with a dial tone.
- He gives them the wrong information.
- He tells them that he must check to see if the person you want to speak to is in, then asks their name, then comes back and tells them that the person to whom they wish to speak is unavailable.

These are so many ways you can lose a sale, why make it harder on yourself by having your phone answered in an improper or unprofessional manner. There is really no reason for it, either.

If we make an assumption that everyone we hire is in sales, no matter what their job function is, we will include some component in our new-hire training that sets them up for success. We can train every employee to understand that every time the phone rings, it is bringing sales into the company, no matter what the call is about. This means that raises, bonuses, and other benefits all go up when enough phone calls are handled using proper phone etiquette.

Let's look at the list above and see how to solve some of the problems.

- *Never answered.* If there is no one to answer the phone, or you are a one-person company and are too busy to answer the phone, then hire a phone answering service.
- *Options Have Changed.* No, they have not. And if you are going to use this ruse to get them to listen to all the options, then do it in your voice, or an employee's voice. Use a different script, too. "Thanks for calling Yuloff Creative. We have several awesome options for you, and here they are . . . ."
- *Machine Voice.* When I get these, I think "Are they still in business? Did I call the right number? Why are they so unprofessional?"
- *The Operator from Hell.* The person you hire to answer the phone *must* speak in a proper tone. Even if they answer the phone two hundred times a day, it must be stressed that the next call could be the most important call of the day. There is a joke that is used when someone makes a very silly error that goes, "You had *one job.*" Yes, they have one job and I hate to say it, but someone has to tell them if they answer the phone poorly. If it can't be corrected, they do not belong working for you in that capacity.
- *Transfers.* They *must* be familiar with every department in the company. If you lose business because a call was transferred improperly, it is not the receptionist's fault. It is bad training. Create a chart labelled, "Why people call us," or "Who does what," so they can just look at the chart and direct the call properly.
- *Premature Hang-ups.* Once again, the person at the front *must* be shown how to use the system.
- *Wrong Information.* "You know what, sir, I do not know who handles that at the company. I have been instructed that when that happens I am supposed to connect you with Ms. X because she knows everything about the company and will satisfy your needs. May I transfer you to her?" Then the receptionist must also follow up to get the correct answer for the future.
- *The person is not in.* Have the receptionist be honest. If you are taking calls, take calls. If you are not taking calls, take *no* calls. Tell the receptionist that you have instructed him that you are going to be in back to back meetings but will be checking for messages at the top of every hour and returning calls. Then return them.

The easiest way to make certain that the phone is answered with proper phone etiquette is to use a *script*. Tell your employees, "This is the exact manner in which to answer the phone." Let them know that they will be secret shopped to make sure that they are doing it correctly. When hiring for the receptionist position, part of your interview should be to go through a mock session of answering your phones.

Have the person answering the phone (or everyone who may answer) create a list of questions that may not have come up during training so that you can both learn together. My first job was working at Thrifty Drug Store in Los Angeles. I was one of those who had to answer the phone and figured out that most of the phone calls that came in after 5 p.m. (we were open until 10 p.m.) were asking what time we were open until so they could get to the pharmacy to pick up their meds or the liquor department on their way home. I began answering the phone with, "Thank you for calling Thrifty Drug Store, Encino, we're open until 10 p.m. this evening. How may I help you?" Most of the time, the response I received was, "Wow, thank you so very much." Click. My manager heard me, noticed how little time I was on the phone, and it became store policy to begin answering the customer's question before they even had to ask it.

When hiring for the receptionist position, part of your interview should be to have them answer your calls. Give them a few tests. And for goodness sake, make sure you call their references from past jobs (as we discussed in chapter 2).

Epilogue
Resources for Your HR Department

There is a lot of professional help to assist in establishing and running a human resources department for your company, both online and offline.

The site—BLR (http://hr.blr.com) offers compliance tools for HR professionals. They offer a free trial. The Society for Human Resource Management, the professional organization for human resource professionals, can be found at https://www.shrm.org.

Offline, you can contact labor law attorneys or professional employment organizations (PEOs). This was one of my favorite resources during my tenure in HR. For the cost of hiring an assistant for me, I convinced my employer to bring on a whole team of professionals to help with employment law and benefits. In fact, because they could offer us discounted benefits given the numbers of employees within their group, they cost my employer less than hiring a full-time assistant for me. We interviewed several and wound up working with two of them (although there are many others): Insperity (http://www.insperity.com) and CPEhr—still my personal favorite (http://www.cpehr.com).

You will find many more resources and templates in the appendices of this book. If you are working with a PEO or labor-law attorney, ask them for the templates that they use to help you customize your tools. If you do not have a professional, feel free to use our sample items (or the links to sample items).

One Last Message

We hope you found value and guidance in these pages. Our mission with this book was to serve you and make a positive difference in your life, your business, and your team.

Our hope is that you found the resources you need to be the leader your team deserves.

Whether you achieve your dreams and goals is solely up to you. No one can promise or guarantee what level of success you, or your team, will achieve.

If we have left you with questions, please send them to us and we'll respond as quickly as possible (info@YuloffCreative.com).

Again, congratulations!

Sharyn and Hank Yuloff

Appendices

The resources and templates here are developed from many sources. In every case, if you are working with a PEO or an employment-law attorney, please ask for their help in customizing their template.

Appendix A

Sample Resumé Scoresheet

APPLICANT INTERVIEW RATING SHEET Position: General Office Support Staff Applicant name: _____		
Questions (Allow 20-30 minutes)	**Comments**	**1-low, 6-high**
Secretarial Skills 1. Using past work experience, discuss how you might handle a situation where you are asked to do several tasks at the same time to meet staff needs.		1-2-3-4-5-6
2. What kind of supervision have you had in the past and how have you responded to it?		1-2-3-4-5-6
3. Your reception duties will call for you to hand numerous questions from students and staff. How would you handle questions that go beyond your knowledge?		1-2-3-4-5-6
Interpersonal Skills 4. Drawing from past work experience, describe several situations where you had to interact with "difficult people" and how you handled the situations.		1-2-3-4-5-6
5. Comment on the following: "Students are the most important people in our business."		1-2-3-4-5-6
6. This office is many times "all things to all people." How do you see your skills and personality fitting into that expectation?		1-2-3-4-5-6
Professional Ethics/Behavior 7. Tell us how you have handled past work situations that required "confidentiality." How might that procedure impact this office?		1-2-3-4-5-6

8. Discuss your understanding of the word "teamwork" and how you have been involved with that process on the job or in other settings. How might teamwork (or lack of it) affect an office setting?		1-2-3-4-5-6
9. Due to student needs and staff schedules, your daily schedule will change occasionally to help in meeting those needs. Comment on your flexibility with time and any expectations you might have.		1-2-3-4-5-6
Closing 10.Do you have any questions of us about this position? THANK YOU! (Describe remaining process.)		
	Total Score:	

Evaluator signature: _____

Appendix B
Sample Phone Interview Template

Here is the phone interview script that I developed:

Before we begin, I do want to ask that you *not* share any proprietary information that you may have gained from previous employment. Especially, if we discuss any specific accomplishments as they must not include any dangerous details that would violate any confidentiality agreement you may have previously signed.

Why are you leaving your current position?

Do they know you are looking?

What are you looking for in your next position?

Where in your career do you hope to be in five to ten years from now?

What do you already know about our company?

What is your definition of an (*job title*) title?

How long do you expect it would take you to make a meaningful contribution to the team?

What most attracts you about this position?

What least attracts you about this position?

What can you do for us that no one else can?

What important trends do you see in this industry?

In your present/last position, what features do/did you like the *most*?

In your present/last position, what features do/did you like the *least*?

In your present/last position, what are/were your five most significant accomplishments?

Had you ever thought of leaving this position before? If yes, what kept you there?

Describe for me your ideal supervisor.

Describe for me a situation when your work was criticized.

What other types of positions and companies are you considering?

What words would your *supervisor* use to describe you?

What words would your *colleagues* use to describe you?

Since we all try to put our best foot forward, describe for me a situation where you had to make something seem better than it really was:

What hour or day restrictions do you have, if any?

What are your compensation requirements?

Do you have any other questions for me?

Is there anything else I should know about you that you haven't had the chance to share as part of this conversation?

Appendix C

Sample Offer Letter

Always Use Letterhead

DATE:

NAME

VIA

Dear **NAME**:

I am pleased to extend the following offer for you to join LEGAL COMPANY ENTITY and its affiliates (collectively "The Company"), subject to verification of credentials and background check (including but may not be limited to verification of eligibility to work in the United States, employment reference verification and criminal background and credit checks). If this offer is acceptable, please execute this letter and return it to us before the close of business on **DATE**.

Title/Position:	**TITLE** (pursuant to the attached Job Description)
Start Date:	**DATE @ TIME**
Base Salary:	This is a *non-exempt* position, payable at *$XX,000.00* annually and *$XXXX* per hour for any over time (hours worked after 8 hours in any work day) paid semi-monthly on or about the 15th and 30th of each month.

Discretionary Bonus: Eligible to receive an annual bonus, up to **XX** percent (**XX**%) of your annual salary, and subject to individual, business unit and company performance. The bonus may be prorated and payable after the first quarter of each calendar year. This bonus is discretionary, and The Company reserves the right and discretion to decide whether or not a bonus will be paid, amount, and any qualifying criteria.

401(k) Plan Employee Contribution:

Eligible to participate after ninety (90) days of full time employment prior to the next entry date, currently calendared for July/January 20**XX**.

401(k) Plan Employer Contribution:

Eligibility to participate in Employer contribution, at The Company's sole discretion, to employee's 401(k) plan commences upon the first year anniversary of employment.

Benefits:

Medical/Dental Insurance:	The Company pays for each employee; dependent coverage paid by the employee
Vacation:	Up to 10 days/year
Sick Days:	Up to 5 days/year
Personal Days:	Up to 2 days/year
Parking:	Paid

At Will Employment: You agree that your employment with The Company constitutes "at will" employment, which means that either you or The Company may terminate the employment relationship at any time, with or without cause or notice. Nothing in this letter shall be construed as an employment contract obligating The Company (expressly or implicitly) to employ you for any specified period of time. While you may receive promotions, commendations, pay raises and the like, this "at will" employment relationship will never change except through a written contract for a specified term signed by you and The Company.

Entire Agreement: This letter, along with the Policies and Procedures Handbook, contain all of the agreements and understandings regarding your employment and the obligations of The Company in connection with employment.

Introductory Period: It is The Company's policy to begin employment with a ninety (90) day introductory period. This gives us both a chance to see if the relationship is mutually beneficial. Prior to the end of the introductory period, we will meet to discuss how to proceed.

This offer is the entire offer to you. There are no other express or implied promises, representations or contracts being offered to you. If you agree to accept this offer, please sign and return this document to our Office & HR Manager, XX, via fax, concurrently mailing the original. A copy of the fully executed version will be provided to you on your start date. I believe you will make an outstanding contribution to The Company and I look forward to working with you!

Sincerely,

NAME
Hiring Manager's Title Here

AGREED TO AND ACKNOWLEDGED BY:

NAME(S) _____   **DATE** _____

JOB DESCRIPTION

Title: **TITLE**

Primary Responsibilities:
- **XXXXX**

Reports to: **TITLE**

Annual Review: **TITLE**

Salary &
Bonus Range: Competitive (\$**XX**,000 - \$**XX**,000 base, 0 − **XX**% discretionary bonus potential)

Qualifications:
- Minimum BA/BS, or comparable experience in related field;
- Computer literate in at least Windows, and MS Office specifically Word, Excel, Outlook and Power Point;
- General knowledge of business and corporate procedures;
- Proficient typing and organizational skills;
- Able to multitask;
- Excellent communication and interpersonal skills are essential;
- Ability to maintain confidentiality at all times is critical;
- Self-starter, professional, and organized; and
- Must be able to work in a highly collaborative, team-oriented framework.

Responsibilities include, but may not be limited to:
- **XX**
- Perform additional miscellaneous assignments per **TITLE's** direction; and
- Continually expand your computer skills and knowledge of INDUSTRY's practices to better the efficiency and productivity of this position.

All employees must comply with firm policies outlines in The Company's Policies and Procedures Manual.

<u>Description of Duties and Specific Responsibilities</u>: **XXXXXXX**

<u>Advancement</u>: Advancement is solely at the discretion of The Company's **TITLE**. The next position is **TITLE (ABBREVIATION)**. The **TITLE** promoted to **TITLE** will

need to have proven competency in all, or in certain circumstances, most, of the areas described above plus:

1.   ability to **XXXXX**.

Appropriate business attire is required: Formal business-wear for meetings external to the office (unless otherwise notified) and business casual dress for the office (unless otherwise notified).

Usual workday: Monday through Friday, 8:30 a.m. to 5:30 p.m. and other times as needed.

I understand that my signature below attests to my understanding of the above job description and to my willingness and ability to perform the above duties consistently and on time.

Name: **NAME**

_____

Signature

Date: _____

cc: Personnel File

Appendix D

Sample Review Template

Annual Review Template
EMPLOYEE'S NAME
DATE

List all the attendees:

1. **Thank you for your service this year**!

2. **Immediate Supervisor will mention at least 1 thing Employee has done in the past year that really stood out.**

3. **Immediate Supervisor will review the Employee's prior goals and list the goals they would like to see achieved in the coming year, keeping in mind the business unit's needs for growth as well as the Employee's;**

90 Day goals:
   i.   XX
   ii. XX
   iii. XX

YYYY goals:
   i.   XX
   ii. XX
   iii. XX
   iv. XX
   v.   XX

4. **Immediate Supervisor will ask: "How can we help you do even better in the coming year?"**

5. **Immediate Supervisor will ask: "Is there anything else you'd like to discuss?"**

6. **Compensation discussions will occur in December of every year.**

Initials: ____ ____
                    ER   EE

Appendix E

Sample Document Resources

Resources to Build Your Employee Handbook

FormSwift will walk you through how to create a free, state compliant, employee handbook.
https://formswift.com/employee-handbook

The SBA (Small Business Administration) offers tips on what to include in your handbook.
https://www.sba.gov/starting-business/hire-retain-employees/employee-handbooks

Rocket Lawyer will also walk you through your state-compliant free employee handbook.
https://www.rocketlawyer.com/form/employee-handbook.rl#/

SHRM (Society for Human Resource Management) offers a free handbook template for members.
https://www.shrm.org/resourcesandtools/tools-and-samples/pages/employee-handbooks.aspx

Sample Disciplinary Action Templates

BYU's (Brigham Young University) sample disciplinary action form is in Microsoft Word, so it is completely editable for your use.
https://view.officeapps.live.com/op/view.aspx?src=https://hr.byuh.edu/sites/hr.byuh.edu/files/hrforms/staffadmindiscaction.doc

Entrepreneur Magazine has as sample notice of disciplinary action in an editable form as well.
http://forms.entrepreneur.com/collections/employee-communication/notice-of-disciplinary-action

Template.net offers more than twenty sample disciplinary letter templates.

https://www.template.net/business/hr-templates/disciplinary-letter/
The Balance provides samples of written reprimands.
https://www.thebalance.com/written-reprimand-sample-1917916

Sample Termination Documentation

The Balance provides sample termination letters.
https://www.thebalance.com/sample-termination-letters-for-the-work-place-1919119

Smartsheet offers an employee termination documentation template.
https://www.smartsheet.com/solutions/employee-termination-documentation

Workable offers an employment termination sample letter (termination for cause).
https://resources.workable.com/employment-termination-letter-for-cause

Rocket Lawyer offers a state-specific free termination letter template.
https://www.rocketlawyer.com/form/termination-letter.rl#/

Sample Exit Interview Documentation

Microsoft Office Live offers a free exit interview template in Microsoft Word.
https://view.officeapps.live.com/op/view.aspx?src=http://hr.ofm.wa.gov/sites/default/files/documents/Strategic%20HR/Workforce%20Planning/ExitInterviewTemplate.doc

The Balance provides sample exit interview questions and suggestions for conducting the exit interview.
https://www.thebalance.com/perform-exit-interviews-1919341

Sample Employment Separation Agreements

All Law provides a separation agreement and general release template.
http://www.calcpa.org/~/media/members/committees%20sections/map%20committee%20information/files/seperation%20agreements/sep_general.pdf?la=en

NJSACOP (New Jersey State Association of Chiefs of Police) offers a separation agreement and a general release sample.
http://www.njsacop.org/rc_files/356/NJSACOP%20separation%20agreement%20template.pdf

Sample Severance Agreements

Fit Small Business offers a **free severance agreement template as a Microsoft Word document and as a PDF.**
 http://fitsmallbusiness.com/severance-agreement-template/

Up Counsel provides a free severance agreement template you can download.
https://www.upcounsel.com/severance-agreement

Panda Doc also offers a severance agreement template.
https://www.pandadoc.com/severance-agreement-template/

One CL offers many free customizable severance forms. http://contracts.one-cle.com/type/38.shtml

Appendix F

Government Resources

FLSA Resources

SHRM (Society for Human Resource Management): FLSA overtime rule resources
https://www.shrm.org/resourcesandtools/legal-and-compliance/employment-law/pages/flsa-overtime-rule-resources.aspx

DOL (Department of Labor): FLSA resource for employers
https://www.dol.gov/whd/foremployers.htm

DOL FLSA Resource by industry
https://www.dol.gov/whd/industry.htm

OSHA Ergonomic Guidelines

IRMI: The new OSHA ergonomics program standard
https://www.irmi.com/articles/expert-commentary/new-osha-ergonomics-program-standard

DOL's OSHA site on ergonomics
https://www.osha.gov/SLTC/ergonomics/

DOL's OSHA site on hazards
https://www.osha.gov/SLTC/ergonomics/controlhazards.html

Appendix G

Sample Expense Reimbursement Report

(including mileage)

Smartsheet: Free expense report templates
https://www.smartsheet.com/free-expense-report-templates

Microsoft Office: Expense report template available for download
https://templates.office.com/en-us/Expense-report-TM00000029

Microsoft Office: Mileage log and expense report
https://templates.office.com/en-us/Mileage-log-and-expense-report-TM02804950

Vertex 42: Travel expense report template for download in Microsoft Excel
https://www.vertex42.com/ExcelTemplates/excel-expense-report.html

Vertex42: Business mileage tracker for download in Microsoft Excel
https://www.vertex42.com/ExcelTemplates/mileage-tracking.html

Appendix H

Other Resources You'll Find Helpful in Managing HR

Dealing with Emergencies

Disaster preparedness
https://www.sba.gov/content/disaster-preparedness

Emergency Response teams
http://www.fema.gov/community-emergency-response-teams

Safety Plans
http://www.blr.com/safetytips/safety-plans

Discrimination

ADA
http://www.futureofprivacy.org/fpf-list-of-federal-anti-discrimination-laws/

HIPPA
http://www.hhs.gov/hipaa/for-individuals/employers-health-information-workplace/index.html

Laws on harassment
http://www.eeoc.gov/laws/types/harassment.cfm

Nolo
http://www.nolo.com/legal-encyclopedia/federal-antidiscrimination-laws-29451.html

Labor Relations

"At Will" explained
http://www.nolo.com/legal-encyclopedia/employment-at-will-definition-30022.html

Employment Practices Liability Insurance (EPLI)
http://www.businessinsurancenow.com/employment-practices-liability/

Federal posters
https://www.dol.gov/general/topics/posters

FLSA
governed by the US Department of Labor (https://www.dol.gov/whd/flsa)

FMLA
(https://www.dol.gov/general/topic/benefits-leave/fmla)

NLRA
https://www.nlrb.gov/resources/national-labor-relations-act

OSHA
https://www.osha.gov

Uniformed Services Employment and Reemployment Rights Act (USERRA)
http://www.dol.gov/elaws/userra.htm
http://www.military.com/benefits/military-legal-matters/userra/userra-frequent-ly-asked-questions.html

Visas
http://travel.state.gov/content/visas/english.html
http://travel.state.gov/content/visas/english/employment.html
http://travel.state.gov/content/visas/english/employment/temporary.html
http://travel.state.gov/content/visas/english/immigrate/employment.html

Compensation
IRS rules on employee vs consultant
https://www.irs.gov/newsroom/understanding-employee-vs-contractor-designation

Mileage allowance
https://www.irs.gov/uac/newsroom/2016-standard-mileage-rates-for-business-medi-cal-and-moving-announced

Wage and Hour investigation
https://www.irs.gov/newsroom/understanding-employee-vs-contractor-designation

Privacy Laws
http://topics.hrhero.com/privacy-laws-for-employees-and-employers/#
http://wwwblr.com/HR-Employment/HR-Administration/Privacy
https://hbr.org/2002/01/selling-the-brand-inside

California Specific Resources
California business resources
http://www.calbizcentral.com

http://business.ca.gov/StartaBusiness/AdministeringEmployees/EqualEmploymentOpportunityLaws/AtWillEmployment.aspx
http://www.calaborlaw.com/can-my-boss-fire-me-at-any-time-for-any-reason-what-is-%E2%80%9Cat-will%E2%80%9D/

"Department of One" Resources
HR Audit
http://www.lexology.com/library/detail.asp?g=843da69f-95b9-4da0-8303-6e3b7dc3815d

Essential HR Metrics
http://business.simplicable.com/business/new/70-HR-metrics-with-examples

Society for Human Resource Management (SHRM)
https://www.shrm.org/hr-today/news/hr-magazine/pages/1115-hr-department-of-one.aspx
https://www.shrm.org/resourcesandtools/tools-and-samples/hr-qa/pages/whatisanhraudit.aspx

Two of the best articles I have read are:
https://blog.apspayroll.com/one-person-hr-department
https://www.entrepreneur.com/article/275284

About the Authors

When it comes to getting expert help for one's business, Hank and Sharyn Yuloff come to you with a very unique perspective. He has a more than thirty-year background in advertising, marketing and public relations. She is an online marketing and human resources expert.

This blend of skills means that they figure out everything from discovering your most profitable demographics, to creating effective messaging and tactics, to solving employee issues.

Their company, Yuloff Creative Marketing Solutions (www.YuloffCreative.com), is a complete marketing services firm, offering traditional and technological marketing plans for small companies. They have been called "a marketing incubator, helping small business owners create a marketing path, then guiding them along that road to success."

Twice yearly, they hold a marketing bootcamp intensive for small groups of businesses owners. Availability for acceptance at the intensive can be found by contacting them through their website.

They have authored five books on marketing, and they host a weekly marketing-tips radio show (www.TheMarketingChecklist.com). They were featured as marketing expert presenters in an entrepreneurial video series with Brian Tracy filmed in 2016, and were selected "America's #1 Coaching Team for Small Business Marketing."

Other Books by Naked Book Publishing

49 Stupid Things People Do with Business Cards . . .
And How to Fix Them

The Marketing Checklist: 80 Simply Ways to Master Your Marketing

The Marketing Checklist 2: 49 More Simple Ways to Master
Your Marketing

The Marketing Checklist 3: Social Media Marketing

And more in the pipeline as well!

SMALL BUSINESS
HUMAN RESOURCES
SECRETS

"Share This Book"

Retail $14.95

Special Quantity Discounts

5-20 Books	$13.95
21-99 Books	$11.50
100-499 Books	$10.25
500-999 Books	$8.95
1000+ Books	$6.95

To Place Your Order Contact:
(800)705-4265
Info@YuloffCreative.com
www.Yuloff Creative .com

Want More Training?

**N̶o̶ ̶M̶o̶r̶e̶
B̶u̶s̶i̶n̶e̶s̶s̶
B̶l̶i̶n̶d̶e̶r̶s̶**

**Getting You
Focused for
Success**

Hank and Sharyn Yuloff
*share their secrets on how to
create your own marketing plan...*
AND THEY'RE THERE TO COACH YOU!

The Small Business
MARKETING✓PLAN

**The D.I.Y. Marketing Plan
with a Coaching Program**

Hours of video with a complete action guide that creates your plan.	Private Facebook Group to network and have your questions answered.	PLUS: Your favorite Non-Profit receives a copy of the plan.

INCLUDES a BONUS 6-HOUR LIVE
SOCIAL MEDIA TRAINING VIDEO

Do your business a favor and take the time to enroll now

TheSmallBusinessMarketingPlan.com

92333982R00062

Made in the USA
San Bernardino, CA
31 October 2018